SOUL FLAME

RISSY SMITH

ISBN: 9798373555692

DEDICATION

To the soul that ignites the flames, you have forever changed my depth of love. You cast a light on all the shadows and strengthen my trust in my intuition. I have always known you my love. I have waited so patiently, even when I thought I'd give up. I still had faith.

-Simply Yours

Note from the author

I have tossed together poems, they have no time-line or order. Please enjoy them in the way your soul calls you to experience my emotions of love and the passion that ensues. Fair warning, sometimes it can get a little steamy!!!

Thank you for letting me into your space, for just this moment.

FROM JUST A THOUGHT

When you think of me, my heart stops and an amazing tingling sensation tickles my crown. It feels like goosebumps on my soul.

I wonder if you know how you effect me. Do you know when and how you touch me? How is it that a tingle can set a blaze of fire through me as though you are inside of me and I am riding the waves of you. I want to scream out I want to call your name as though it were the answer to my prayer. This silent call of love to end it all.

You make love to my soul, and I'm lost. I want every part of you with me, on me, in me. Tasting me, experiencing all that I am. As though I only exist for this, for you, forever.

FATE

The memory is sweet and so refined
I find myself reaching back in time,
Holding on to touch the light within,
The answer to the darkness that threatens to win.
Only one has known this path,
And fought to hold on through life's naked wrath,
But she is the mist that surrounds my soul,
Longing to touch her has taken its toll.
I feel the blanket of her embrace,
Yet I cannot see nor touch her face.
So I lie in reverie so long in wait,
Blessed because she was my fate.

TRUE HEART

From my first breath, 'til the break of present day,
I have loved only one, for whom I pray.
Beyond the barriers of rhyme or reason,
My love for you knows no season.
Your true heart has touched me with the warmth of its light,
And sparked a fire within I will no longer fight.
Hear this heart that beats anew,
And claim the soul destined for you.

SHINE

In your eyes, the truth I see,
The soul within is calling me.
Bring forth the wish of love unbidden,
These gifts, so long you've hidden.
The magic within it begs to unveil,
The source of your greatest tale.
I stand before you, my hands upon your chest,
With a wish to lie my head, to finally rest.
The echoes of home resound from your core,
I'm so lost, I beg for more.
The sound of your voice calling my name,
Creates a fire only a touch could tame.
Hold me close, embrace my light,
For you alone, I shine tonight.

CONSENT

I feel your pull across the divide,
Like ebb and flow, your passion I ride.
With just a taste of your souls desire,
A spark has ignited an infinite fire.
Your thoughts are dancing upon my skin,
As your demand for pleasure pulses within.
Like a wave your command covers me,
I'm caught in the depths of your fantasy.
Release is calling, I beg to know,
When you'll consent to lose control.

PASSION UNLEASHED

I feel you in the silent moments of each day,
As a deep yearning that promises to have its way.
If only I could get you here before me,
I'd show you just what you've done to me.
These cravings for you have me coming undone,
Love, I promise, you are the only one.
The one that I taste as my eyes close each night,
That slumbers inside of this souls light.
A passion unleashed, I can't deny,

SWITCH

Sometimes I think about sitting you in a chair, asking you to trust me, to close your eyes…
I find myself walking around the chair leaning in behind you, lifting your locs, leaning down so slowly.. inhaling the scent of you….whispering into your neck all of the things your vulnerability is doing to me. I feel the power buried within, it is so intoxicating….I can't stop my fingers from tracing the nape of your neck down between your shoulder blades, softly…I won't stop until your skin craves my touch, and your body moves toward me, to intensify the connection… Mine…
Walking to the front of you, I lean down and press my lips to your forehead holding your face in my hands, my lips stay just long enough for you to feel the heat in my kiss. … trailing kisses to your neck, the pulse of your life is so intense beneath my lips that I can no longer keep myself from running my mouth along your jaw, and down your throat….I sigh and give in to the magic of you….kneeling down in front of you, kissing your collar bone, can you feel my lips tracing your skin? Open your eyes and look at me love, do you see the fire within? I'm not in control, you have the power. You sit before me, but it is me that is bare before you. Will you end the connection or will you take what is yours?

DESTINY

Kisses lost upon the wind,
Reality teases to rescind.
Intimate moments I've held so long,
Searching for this love so strong.
Kneeling down these years I've prayed,
Of the soul that destiny made.
One perfect soul split in two,
Never to love anyone so true.
Caresses soft across my skin,
Eternity's promise I hold within.

NAUGHTY OR COMPLIANT

The door clicks shut, and I hold my breath as you walk towards the room. Your footsteps stop, then I hear the note I left you on the table rustle. Now you are walking to the bedroom door. Smiling, I count away the seconds, knowing that you are just on the other side of the door, taking off each piece of clothing. I know that I will be waiting for a bit, because you are so careful in how you disrobe. I picture each button that your fingers maneuver slide through the buttonhole. With each one opened, I can picture more and more of your skin being revealed. You take your time with each one that you loosen because you know that I am envisioning it all. I take a deep breath in and continue my imagining the rise and fall of your chest with each breath. My heart stops as I hear the zipper of your slacks slide, the zip down is so slow; this is sweet torture. I picture your shirt draped open, the button on your slacks gaping. You look down at your skin and lick your lips thinking about what I'm going through. I see that, all of it. The vision of you has me burning up. Will you continue to remove everything like I requested? Or will you let the thought of what I have promised you push you through the door? Naughty or compliant, what will it be?

LEAP OF FAITH

Take the leap,
Your heart is mine to keep.
As my sun sets, we are opposite,
As your moon rises, we are infinite.
The soul destined for you,
The reality of one from two.
If you fall, I feel the pain,
Mirroring you, I've felt insane.
Wanting to shout, but silenced with fear,
So many words I've longed to hear.
All you are, is part of me,
Awaken love it's time to see.
A life that's waiting for your first breath,
For a fated love, that knows no death.

STORY TIME

Click, and the knob is turning,
The door is opening, and all I can see is your shadow. Your shadow against the door frame, and the sound of your breath.
Biting my lip, I take in a slow breath and just wait. Wait for you to completely enter, completely see, and completely understand what I'm willing to give.
My back is facing you as you walk in; it is bare. Kneeling on the floor with the palms of my hands on my knees, I can feel the vibration on the floor of each step you take towards me.
My breath hitches as the floggers' tails lightly caress my thighs as you pull it towards you.
My favorite choice, and instantly the heat between my thighs is enhanced.
Before I can even formulate a thought, the tails of the flogger teasingly cross my back, and then they become solid steady slashes.
My head is bowed, and I am counting each lash.
You will ask how many,, and I will respond because I am always a good girl.
Seventeen at last count, and I'm aching to be touched.
Will it be punishment you seek when you place your hand between my legs and find the evidence of my surrender?

STORY TIME

SURRENDER SURRENDER

Love, I can fight no more,
Destiny has brought me to your door.
In a word, you are home,
In your eyes, I've always known.
The need to stand against your chest,
To finally know what it is to rest.
This need I feel defies reason,
For it knows no season.
My dreams so rich with your desire,
Awaken within me a constant fire.
My touch is not enough to set me free,
Surrender, I surrender willingly.

FANTASIES

Indulging in thoughts of you is a constant high,
Fantasies start with my hands on your thigh.
Trailing my fingers across your skin,
I watch as they part, and invite me in.
Ooh, you're watching and biting your lip,
Now the control has started to slip.
Reigning in this need to devour,
Every inch of your sexual power.
I place my hands beneath your hips,
And pull you closer to my lips.
A promise is granted upon my exhale,
In this, in you, I will never fail.

SAY I CAN

Say I can, I beg into the air,
Thoughts of you pulling my hair.
The rise and fall of this tide,
Tossing my head side to side.
Visions of hand to thigh
Parting for you, awaiting your reply.
Say I can, whisper in my ear,
The very words I long to hear.
Of how you want to see me fall
Of your desire to have it all.
My request is but a momentary release,
For you alone I want to please.

PROMISED TO YOU

Love is reaching and carries you through,
All of life's turmoil and sad days too.
You my heart, are loves' beautiful note,
The reason behind my hearts faith in hope.
Love is never binding or cruel to a soul,
It is meant to flow and to make you whole.
Be free to laugh on the wind,
For Love has promised to rescind.
Anything meant to bring you down,
You are meant to wear Gods crown.
For love will lead you to the light,
Where all darkness fades from sight.
You are perfect as you are,
Never question your love thus far.
Take my hand, I'll lead you through,
Forever my love is promised to you.

DREAM LOVER

Deep sigh, this distance is taking a toll,
Even in my sleep you consume my soul.
Your breath warm against my skin,
Captures me as you pull me in.
Oh sweet torture, the scent of you teases me so,
Breathing you in, I lose control.
Focusing now, I beg to prolong my time,
The only moment I can call you mine.
So close Love, your trailing fingers I open to invite,
Please God let it be this night.
Having been denied this moment so long,
Waking now would be so wrong.
Dream Lover, I need to feel,
The depth of your loving, make it real.
And dive you do, to my very core,
Pleasure I feel from every pore.
Surrender takes me under her tide,
And washes over me as I ride.
Chasing now my need so vast
Wakefulness is rising fast.
To whom will the victory go?
Eyes wide, guess we'll never know.

ETERNITY

Waking this morning, the words trail,
I'm coming for you, reverberations of all that can entail.
Words whispered along my conscious mind,
Shaking me with intentions to bind.
My soul is dancing as you reach for me,
Take me now and set me free.
One touch contains what you desire to know,
Fear not love, forever is in the seeds you sow.
Creation of you starts and ends in me,
For we are love for all eternity.

WHY CHOOSE

Passion is all I see in your eyes,
Fear keeps you behind the ties.
You touch me with your mind,
Fearing what in reality you will find.
Fantasies and dreams carry me through,
But in truth you long for the view.
Of how thoughts of you cause me to linger,
On the very parts you hunger to finger.
Aww yes love I see you, I do
Do you feel what you bring me to?
Can you hear me whisper your name,
When I'm begging for surrender with no blame?
For you are all I want, day and night,
Pleading for your touch to make it right.
No one but you can fill my heart,
And you've known this from the start.
Why choose, when you can have it all,
The decision was made when I answered your call.
I chose you without fear that you'd deny,
What you know in your heart is no lie.

DAYDREAMS

Daydreams start with you entering my door,
Pulling me close, taking me to the floor.
The time has come, you've waited so long,
To taste this life, how can it be wrong.
I feel your heat across my chest,
As you run your hand across my breast.
Arching my back to encourage the flow,
Praying for you to take it slow.
Caress me as though this is no race,
Kiss me deep and savor the pace.
Promises fall from my lips,
As you part my legs and roll your hips.
Yours, my energy take what you need,
Your appetite is what I desire to feed.
Fill me with the light of your soul,
Push until I lose control.
Make me beg for that needed kiss,
The center of me longs for this.
Caresses of your tongue upon my core,
Take my breath, I want more.
I want to feel you lose all inhibition,
As you satisfy my needy condition.

CAN YOU

I am so in love with you,
I feel you when you don't think I do.
Can you feel the love I send,
Or my words that this love has no end?
Can you see my movement along this conscious plane,
Do you see how the need for you drives me insane?
I want to lay beneath the weight of your soul,
Grinding until we become whole.
Kissing the depths of yesterday into tomorrow,
Washing away every pain, every sorrow.
For you are love and I it's home,
Infinite places for you to roam.
Expand your light to encompass the moon,
Forever cannot come too soon.

DO YOU

Prolonged thoughts of you are tearing me apart.
Wanting your kiss upon my neck is just the start.
Tell me love, can you hear my thoughts, do they show?
How I want to straddle your thighs and kiss you slow.
I can feel the tingling upon my skin,
And see your vision of pulling me in.
My chest rising and falling with this need,
To give you my soul to feed.
For only you can fill the hunger inside,
My passion for you I will not hide.
Thoughts of you ignite pure fire,
You are my eternal desire.
Do you know I can feel your touch within,
That I can feel your lips across my skin?
Do you know it causes me to moan,
Or when you stop, I beg and grown?
At times I feel your body's release,
A vibration within and all thoughts cease.

CARESS MY THOUGHTS

My mind is open to your deep gaze,
When you walk my mind to find the rays.
The rays of light that feed your thirst,
The love that sets your heart to burst.
Trail the vines and walkways slow,
Everything is yours, you need to know.
When you caress my thoughts the visions clear,
Can you see how you bring me near?
How I move my head side to side,
Grinding against the promised ride.
Do you feel my heart beat moving fast,
Praying aloud to make this last?
Do you see the light between your hand and mine,
Do you see how you make her shine?
This is where you've come from the start,
To offer this soul your surrendered heart.

YOUR SUN

Smile love, for I am your sun.
I am warmth and light that moves as one.
To embrace the darkness and lift your spirit,
Music that rises to please, do you hear it?
The moment I touch you I become real,
With laughter, joy and such love I feel.
Your soul is a beautiful treasure,
Mine, for no other could measure.
Hold me close Love and fill your need,
Take from me what borders on greed.
All that forever calls you to hold,
A love, this love, more precious than gold.

NEED

Longing grips my every thought,
Time moves slowly, in these emotions I've fought.
Seeking your heart is my only desire,
The only answer to this life of fire.
Will your need consume all that is me,
Or will it surrender to fate gracefully?
Questions upon which you can cast sweet light,
Will you illuminate my path this night?
Show me all that you've hidden so deep,
Things you feared, promises you keep.
Share it all I dare you still,
Give me your need, heed my will.

TAKE ME

Woken now, I lie still, no thought,
Pulling the remnants of my dream so hot.
Deep hunger you've left buried deep,
Breath slow the visions seep.
The request to show you my all,
With just your thought the covers fall.
Exposed to you in every way,
My eyes are begging you to stay.
See all to that I have and reach inside,
My body and soul, surrendered I cannot hide.
Only you can see the joy, the light,
Will you take me this night?

I REACH FOR YOU

I reach for you in the dark,
Because your soul left it's mark.
Only you spark the light within,
Guiding a life, ready to begin.
I've waited for this love so deep,
A soul rooted in promises to keep.
Without your heat lying upon my breast,
This anxious heart cannot rest.
For it waits for your magic to weave it's spell,
Longing to hear the words that compel.
Two souls to dance as one,
Until the moon marries the sun.

MY FATE

What am I to do,
When I can only think of you.
How your smile lights the dark that hides away,
Or how I long for you to ask me to stay.
Running is not the answer I seek,
I promise you, my heart's not weak.
My fate is tied to the rhythm and ease
Of the only soul I long to please.
Imperfection runs through my very depth,
Without you there is no breath.
No reason to commit these words to stone,
Or sing a love song that has no tone.
There would be no color in life to see,
If I could not hold you close to me.
The air would swirl its endless dance,
Around my life if it had the chance.
Save me, love me, give me reason,
To exist beyond this lonely season.
Need to wrap your arms around my beating heart,
Because fate has already played it's part.

FEAR

I rise each day bathed in love,
And extend gratitude to God above
I am thankful for the air I breathe,
And pray that all my fears gently leave.
They have tethered themselves for far too long,
Trying to confuse right from wrong.
Love is the purest form of clarity,
Yet fear pushes it away from me.
Not because the love is not returned,
Only that doubt left bridges burned.
Making up stories that you are not real,
So how do I explain the depth I feel?
How thoughts of you light my day,
How I stumble trying to find words to say.
How your joy becomes my fire,
How I pray to give you all you desire.
I fill my cup with the energy you give,
Because your light encourages hope to live.

EPIC PASSION

Angelic the look upon your face,
How I ache for each line to trace.
To feel your breath still with need,
A silent request my soul must feed.
Mesmerized by your lips, a passionate haze,
Watching you run your tongue across, pause, teeth graze.
Can you taste my need across the spanse,
Your eyes are lost in a trance.
Teasing away the momentary pain,
Of wanting you so bad, I must remain.
To build the tension; to make it last,
This epic passion, could burn so fast.
Taking us down the well so deep,
This internal promise I fight to keep.
My soul bargains for a kiss; just one,
My heart is racing to beat the sun.
Just give me a moment to feel your heat,
So that I may live, my heart may beat.
Without your touch I'll cease to be,
Consumed by your fire for eternity.

THE PASSION

ONE WITH YOU

Light dances in your gaze,
A teasing truth that your soul does raise.
The way I feel when you look at me,
My heart stops suddenly.
Your gaze, converses with my heart,
One with you, no end, no start.
I pray that you never look away,
I pray that you need to stay.
Forever falls easily upon your ear,
From this heart that has no fear.
See me in all my light,
As a promise of everything right.
A victory of heart and soul,
A truth that only you can know.

LOVE TRUE

Timeless, my head lying on your thighs,
As you sweep away my bitter cries.
Your touch is tender, caresses so sweet,
You take away the pain of memory's deceit.
The touch of your fingers twisting the strands,
Gentle my soul, creates demands.
A prod, a pull, a screaming need,
To give you a place for your soul to feed.
Time slips by and you have yet to move,
The love I have within, I need to prove.
A simple move puts us face to face,
Giving you access, lines to trace.
Something new for you to see,
This broken soul a hollow me.
A soul that needs to feel it all,
Hold me now before I fall.
I need to feel you in every way,
This hunger for you will always stay.
For you are the meaning of love true,
Please tell me you need me too.

CHANCE

Could you take my thoughts and see me?
A woman who is learning to become a better me?
Rare is the soul that stops to see,
One bloom amongst the sea.
Love is rare from such a glance,
Even so, will you take the chance?

MY OBEDIENCE

I see your lips moving, whispering "Baby,"
Everything in your eyes, promises maybe.
Of how you'll bring me to submission,
Have me pleading for permission.
For the right to earn your pleasure,
My obedience is my only measure.
Eyes down kneeling at your feet,
Patiently waiting for your pain so sweet.
Hot and quick it sears my thigh,
The crop delivers your expected reply.
Open, my legs open on demand,
Hungrily waiting your next command.
You move close and raise my chin,
Giving me direction where to begin.
The scent of you so near is heady,
Swallowing I fight to remain steady.
For all I want is to taste your pleasure,
To be your one and only treasure.
The one your hand grabs to make it slow,
To savor all that my tongue can show.
Relentless, I become to fulfill your desire,
Your moans ignite an internal fire.
Your Satisfaction is what I need,
Punishment later for my endless greed.

SPEAK MY NAME

Your energy surrounds me,
Touching and loving me so sweet.
How intoxicated I am by your scent,
In my soul, I know we are meant.
Meant to thrive, meant to love,
As the wind hints those secrets from above.
Assurances of all that is true,
Acknowledgement is all I beg of you.
For I fear you'll never open the door,
To allow me to give you the love I hear you screaming for.
Close your eyes love and trust my heart,
For a promise of loyalty from the start.
A promise to always bring you the comfort of home,
A feeling I know, that you have never known.
A promise for a smile that never leaves your lips,
For it is the simplest of my amazing gifts.
You'll never have to measure a word,
Because I promise that you will always be heard.
Your words are precious so speak with no blame,
The call of your heart, love, speak my name.

WHAT I MEAN

When I say I want to make love with you, this is what I mean. I want to sit facing you knee to knee. I want to place your hand in mine, and mine in yours. I want to touch my forehead to yours. I want to combine our energies. I want to become one with you. So when you first taste my lips, the sweetness of my soul is what you savor. When your hand caresses my chest, you'll feel my heart beat for the first time. Because when you and I become one. Life begins. I want to feel how our energies move from within and become a whole new entity that lives and breathes as it surrounds us. I want to look into your eyes when you cross my threshold, to see the wonder as you discover my depths. I want to be so close to you, that it feels like we share the same skin, the same blood, the same soul. I want to move you through emotions you've never experienced, just to show you what I mean by I want to make love with you.

BREATHLESS

I see you running along the sand,
Coming close you take my hand.
Pulling us down under the fall,
Seeing your need to give it all.
I pull the turquoise cloth off your skin,
Gasping as I see the beauty within.
Your eyes plead away your need,
Promise you love, from you I'll feed.
I kiss you upon your thigh,
As you part your legs and begin to sigh.
To say you're beautiful does not compare,
To the exquisite sight of your skin bare.
I want to lose myself in the taste of you,
To show you what this need can do.
The need to devour you steady and slow,
The need to please your very soul.
I pull you closer no room to spare,
Your skin and I have much to share.
I'll give this energy until you grind,
And get lost in my kisses kind.
I will not cease til your need is met,
Until you're breathless and thoroughly wet.

SUNFLOWERS

Sensual soul, your eyes they
Scream,
Uncharted the way you command my dream.
Need building a rapturous fire,
Flames growing from my desire.
Love, you are torture so sweet,
Only you, just you know my defeat.
Wake me please before I fall,
Eternity lies within your call.
Ragged my breaths await release,
Still, so still I beg you please.

TODAY

I wake and wonder will this be the day,
The day that you're not the first thought or wish I pray.
A life spent waiting for this love,
The love I've spent lifetimes thinking of.
I've dreamt of moments your lips I touch,
Is wanting this life asking too much?
In dreams I feel the heat of your hand,
Caressing my spirit leaving your brand.
How can I walk through life knowing you this way,
When all I want is for you to stay.
To reach out and pull me close,
To say dear light it's you I chose.
For eternity my heart longs to beat,
Next to yours a sound so sweet.
A thrum that dances within my soul,
Oh this wish, it takes a toll.
So rise I must and face the day,
I'll wait until for me you pray.

MY CALL

Dear Love meet me this night at rest,
Travel the planes of the astral nest.
I miss the feel of breath on my skin,
The way you hold me rides on sin.
The distance between us is rarely kind,
When wanting to taste you plagues my mind.
The sweetest layers that call to me,
To give you love so exquisitely.
I want to hear pleasure falling in sighs,
I want to feel the heat between your thighs.
May I be selfish and claim my need,
Will you surrender and let me lead?
I promise this desire will never fall,
Tell me Love, will you answer my call?

TOO PROUD

Is it selfish to want to be whom you miss,
The one you can't wait to kiss.
The thoughts that's swim up inside,
Of feelings from which you cannot hide.
Delicious ideas to bring me close,
Knowing it was you I chose.
To see the light burn deep within your eyes,
Just by getting to touch my thighs.
To hear me utter your name,
Tell me Love am I too tame?
Should I scream the words aloud,
Have I let my ego become too proud?
For you are whom I miss,
The only lips I long to kiss.
The only smile I want to see,
The only soul for me.

THE WAY TO LOVE

I want to surrender to lose control,
To let your love touch my soul.
I lay here and dream of your hands so strong,
Caressing away every wrong.
I want to feel the heat of your fingers,
Pushing aside any doubt that lingers.
I want to ride your digits without a care,
Until its only pleasure we share.
I want you to feel the trust within,
How my core warms your skin.
I want to scream because you pleasure me so,
But Love I need you to make it slow.
Take me now to the heavens above,
Show me the way to love.

HAVE IT ALL

I cannot sleep, I cannot rest,
When all I want is to lie upon your chest.
To trace the skin that rises and falls,
To hear your heart race when pleasure calls.
The thought is pure heaven to me,
To caress you so lovingly.
When you move beneath my touch,
The pressure I feel is such a rush.
It drives all reason from my mind,
It makes it hard to be kind.
I want to explore and just devour,
Every inch, every hour.
The sun will rise before we fall,
Tell me Love, say I can have it all.

YOU DIDN'T KNOW

No matter the time day or night,
You make this journey take flight.
You are the reason I can or cannot sleep,
This souls journey runs so deep.
I feel your energy hold me when you're feeling low,
That's something I bet you didn't know.
I dream of you loving me 'til the morn,
For this, for you, I was born.
I see our life, how we dance and laugh,
How my calm soothes your wrath.
Oh how the light shines when you look at me,
And how you think you've done it secretly.
I want you to see how I ache,
To tell you I'm yours to take.
For there is no other today, or ever,
A love divine that's impossible to sever.

MY PLEASURE

I picture you waiting for me, kneeling on the bed; black button down opened completely. Just grazing the sides of your thighs. The power of your whole being pulsing within your eyes. The fullness of your breasts heavily seductive, radiating with the desire to be touched.
The scent of your soul calls me forward.
Across your bare lap sits your shiny black leather strap. Ready to put into action, to take what's yours.
Your full lips slightly open, slightly upturned, ready to pronounce your commands.
I close my eyes and touch places only you can see, only you control.
Will you let me lose myself in the desire of pleasing you?
Will you let me come close, let me taste you? Will you allow me my pleasure?
Can you see the pleading in my eyes, for just a taste? How I want to feel your pleasure build? Will you allow your greed to take over, as you take your pleasure from me?
Bind my hands, spark my will, take all that I am or desire to be.
My Pleasure is yours.

DESIRES MISERY

Today, right now I'm on fire
I crave your touch to quench my desire.
The pressure is building so sweet this pain,
My need for you is driving me insane.
Your eyes taunt me and bind my will,
Your power demands and I grow still.
My core is throbbing begging for bliss,
I open my self to your kiss.
Feather soft upon my lips
Held down I rock my hips.
Against your mouth I want to ride,
Whimpering when your fingers slide.
Into the depths, the core of me,
Love I need you desperately.
Take my soul as you bring me near,
Baby cum for me is what I need to hear.
Only you will set me free,
From desires misery.

LIGHT STORM

I feel a distant thunder rolling through

I want to harness the storm that's you.

To be the shore that catches your tide,

Knowing it's my soul you'll ride.

Taking in the brutality of your pain,

A sweet surrender from me you'll gain.

I will not break upon your touch,

Nothing you give will be too much.

For I was made to be your home

To transform your energy like you've never known.

To be the breeze that whispers your name,

A light storm you've longed to tame.

Feed my hunger, one brutal kiss,

Devour my whimpers of pure bliss.

Enforce your will upon my essence so sweet,

Breathe in the scent of my defeat.

THE KEY

My very essence is drifting away,

Lost to the desires we play.

Twisting in this empty bed,

Wanting to match the pictures in my head.

My fingers trail across my skin so sweet,

As my flesh rises in defeat.

Surrendering to a primal need,

A vow of passion I feed.

Every sigh and moan I hold,

A wealth of secrets untold.

Only you possess the key,

To free me so sensually.

SEXUAL HAZE

I can feel the love you pour
It touches the depths of my core.
A tingle across my inward gaze,
Leads me into this sexual haze.
A feeling so intense and rare,
It has me writhing without a care.
Lead me Love to your darkest desire,
For I was made to stoke your fire.
My passion builds with just a thought,
Oh what this love has wrought.
Thoughts of you I can't betray,
Will always make me feel this way.

I CAN

Can you imagine the need to feel so close to someone that you want to crawl into their lap? To lay your head on their shoulder and just breathe them in.

To be so close to someone, that you can't seem to get close enough. To exchange kisses, hugs, and passionate touches. Only to enter into a deep desire to become one whole beating heart.

To reach the level of intimacy where your energy caresses mine, and then completely covers it in protection, then dominance…. Highlighting every nuance from exquisite pain to breathtaking ecstasy.

I can.

MINE

Mine, a smile that sang my soul awake,
A desired kiss that makes me ache.
I want to touch every part before me,
I want to feel this love that defines infinity.
I want to scream when I can't hold you near,
I want to speak my love in words you'll hear.
If just for a moment you could see my heart,
Maybe life wouldn't tear us apart.
Because you are and will always be,
Everything in this universe to me.
Mine since before this life was a spark,
Mine when this world goes dark.

PRECIOUS

A kiss from your lips upon my brow,
Is the only thing I need right now.
Simple the sweet touch defines control,
It removes any pain in my soul.
Tender the grace it falls like rain,
Washing through every vein.
Renewing me to a semblance of me,
The version only the world can see.
In these moments when I fall apart,
You show me the resilience in my heart.
That each crack defines the light,
And shows the beauty in my fight.
That the life within me is precious to you,
That the kiss is something you need too.

SIRE

Know, you know the depths of me,
Keeping the secrets so carefully.
Rise and fall between your sighs,
On my knees, hands to thighs.
Innocent your eyes deceive,
Oh the torture, I desire reprieve.
Slow and steady you lift my gaze,
Needing only to see my praise.
Captured I am by the heat of your fire,
Evermore enchanted by your desire.

ENERGY

I feel all of you when I am still
You pour over me and take my will.
Silent surrender to your touch,
Your love is never too much.
It builds this fire that warms my core,
And has me begging for so much more.
Your whispers ride upon my skin,
Promises of pleasure tease within.
Can you feel the rising tide,
Or how upon your energy I ride?
It's as though you're taking your pleasure,
And it hits me in equal measure.
Release is there I feel your sigh,
As it washes over and leaves me high.

THE AUTHOR

Rissy Smith is a native of Los Angeles, California. She loves spending her time with her collected family. Her definition of family, are the souls that gravitate to one another and create a soul tribe.

She believes in spreading love to one and all. She has a strong belief that no matter what life has thrown at you, you are always capable of seeing your own strength and beauty. That we are that one smile given, that may save a life. That we should all strive to love unconditionally.

www.ingramcontent.com/pod-product-compliance
Lightning Source LLC
LaVergne TN
LVHW050318160826
845677LV00014B/3454

* 9 7 9 8 3 7 3 5 5 5 6 9 2 *